CW01368105

Ancient & modern pictures, and water-colour drawings

Manson & Woods Christie

Nabu Public Domain Reprints:

You are holding a reproduction of an original work published before 1923 that is in the public domain in the United States of America, and possibly other countries. You may freely copy and distribute this work as no entity (individual or corporate) has a copyright on the body of the work. This book may contain prior copyright references, and library stamps (as most of these works were scanned from library copies). These have been scanned and retained as part of the historical artifact.

This book may have occasional imperfections such as missing or blurred pages, poor pictures, errant marks, etc. that were either part of the original artifact, or were introduced by the scanning process. We believe this work is culturally important, and despite the imperfections, have elected to bring it back into print as part of our continuing commitment to the preservation of printed works worldwide. We appreciate your understanding of the imperfections in the preservation process, and hope you enjoy this valuable book.

CATALOGUE

OF

THE VALUABLE COLLECTION

OF

ANCIENT & MODERN

PICTURES

AND

𝔚ater-colour 𝔇rawings

OF

SAMUEL CARTWRIGHT, ESQ.,

Deceased, late of Old Burlington Street:

which (*by Order of the Executors*)

𝔚ill be 𝔖old by 𝔄uction by

Messrs. CHRISTIE, MANSON & WOODS

AT THEIR GREAT ROOMS,

8, KING STREET, ST. JAMES'S SQUARE,

On **FRIDAY, FEBRUARY 26, 1892,**

AT ONE O'CLOCK PRECISELY.

———◆———

May be viewed Two Days preceding, and Catalogues had, at Messrs. Christie, Manson and Woods' Offices, 8, *King Street*, *St. James's Square*, *S.W.*

CONDITIONS OF SALE.

I. THE highest Bidder to be the Buyer, and if any dispute arise between two or more Bidders, the Lot so in dispute shall be immediately put up again and re-sold.

II. No person to advance less than 1s., above Five Pounds, 5s., and so on in proportion.

III. In the case of Lots upon which there is a reserve, the Auctioneer shall have the right to bid on behalf of the Seller.

IV. The Purchasers to give in their Names and Places of Abode, and to pay down 5s. in the pound, or more, in part of payment, or the whole of the Purchase-Money, *if required*, in default of which, the Lot or Lots so purchased to be immediately put up again and re-sold.

V. The Lots to be taken away and paid for, whether genuine and authentic or not, with all faults and errors of description, at the Buyer's expense and risk, within Two days from the Sale, Messrs. CHRISTIE, MANSON and WOODS not being responsible for the correct description, genuineness, or authenticity of, or any fault or defect in, any Lot, and making no warranty whatever.

VI. To prevent inaccuracy in delivery, and inconvenience in the settlement of the Purchases, no Lot can on any account be removed during the time of Sale, and the remainder of the Purchase-Money must absolutely be paid on the delivery.

VII. Upon failure of complying with the above Conditions, the Money deposited in part of payment shall be forfeited, all Lots uncleared within the time aforesaid shall be re-sold by public or private Sale, and the deficiency (if any) attending such re-sale shall be made good by the Defaulter at this Sale.

CATALOGUE.

On FRIDAY, FEBRUARY 26, 1892,

AT ONE O'CLOCK PRECISELY

The following are Sold by order of the Executors of SAMUEL CARTWRIGHT, Esq, deceased, late of Old Burlington Street.

DRAWINGS.

1	A LANDSCAPE, with animals—*body colour*, a chromolithograph, after the Princess Royal's drawing, and Spanish figures at a window	3
2	VIEW NEAR VENICE, a Landscape, and a Road Scene	3
3	VIEWS OF RICHMOND AND CHISWICK—*a pair*	2
4	A SHIPWRECK	
5	A STUDY OF A FEMALE, and a Landscape—*chalk*	2
6	A PAIR OF RIVER SCENES—*sepia*	2
7	VIEWS OF DOVER—*a pair*	2
8	AN ITALIAN FAMILY, after Rowlandson, by Alken	

J ABSOLON

9 THE MISSAL

V W BROMLEY
5 FRIGHTENED BY GEESE

V W BROMLEY.
6 ADMIRATION

A. BUZZI.
7 TOO COLD FOR CHARITY

W. CALLOW
8 A FRENCH HARBOUR SCENE

M. CAZIN.
9 A LANDSCAPE, with cottage

J. M CLAUDE
10 A RIDE ON THE SANDS; and the Companion

D COX.
11 A RIVER SCENE, with a bridge and cows
12 CROSSING THE HEATH
13 KENILWORTH CASTLE

W. W. DEANE.
14 THE GATE OF JUSTICE, Alhambra

W W. DEANE
15 INTERIOR OF SAN MINIATO, Florence

B. EVANS.

16 A River Soene, with rainbow; and a Landscape, with a storm   2

E. GILL, 1880

17 St. Paul's

A. F. GRACE

18 Amberley

A. F GRACE, 1880

19 Amberley

EMIL LESSORE

20 Children, in a landscape   2
21 Turkish Figures at a Door, and Children in a Landscape   2
22 Feeding the Ducks
23 Children, with a dog
24 Children at a Cottage Door
25 Figures; and Cupids   2
26 Children, at the cottage door, and the Companion   2
27 Children, and Ducks and Children—*a pair*   2
28 Blowing Bubbles, and a Girl seated—*a pair*   2
29 Figures in a Garden; and Children with Rabbits   2
30 Children, with a goat, and The Woodgatherer   2

BIRKET FOSTER.
28 A Cottage, with girl and cow

C. GREEN.
29 Mussel Gatherer

L HAGHE
30 Treves

H G. HINE.
31 On the Beach, Great Yarmouth

H G HINE
32 Dorchester Downs

H. G. HINE.
33 Near Lewes, with shepherd and sheep

H G HINE.
34 Downs near Dunstable

H G HINE.
35 Seamer Hill, Sussex

H. G HINE
36 On the Beach, Great Yarmouth

H. HINE

37 A Coast Scene

S. P JACKSON

38 A Coast Scene, with castle

S P JACKSON

39 On the Thames

S. P JACKSON

40 Near Hambledon, on the Thames

J J JENKINS.

41 A Landscape, with cottage and ducks

W L LEITCH.

42 Crossing the Brook

J H LEONARD

43 The Silent Night

D. H McKEWAN

44 The Head of Loch Callater, Aberdeenshire

E MACIRONE

45 A Norman Doorway

W. W MAY

16 OFF DORDRECHT

D H McKEWAN

47 THE LIBRARY AT KNOLE

D H McKEWAN

48 LUDLOW CASTLE

D H McKEWAN.

49 STUDY OF TREES

J. H NIOLE

50 MILL NEAR ESSENFORD, Cornwall

J MOGFORD

51 A COAST SCENE, with fishermen

J MOGFORD

52 THE LAND'S END

J. MOGFORD

53 SEAWEED GATHERERS, on the coast of Normandy

J MOGFORD

54 NORHAM CASTLE, on the Tweed

J ORROCK

55 A MARSH SCENE

A PENLEY.

56 A Harbour Scene, Greece
57 Buttermere Lake
58 Llanrwst Church, on the Conway

SIR J. REYNOLDS (After)

59 The Duchess of Rutland

R R SCANLAN

60 The Sportsman's Luncheon; and a Peasant Girl

G. SHALDERS.

61 Driving Home the Flock

G W SHEPHEARD

62 The Forest of Fontainebleau

W COLLINGWOOD SMITH.

63 A River Scene, with figures

C. VACHER.

64 Blevio, Meggionigo Lago di Como

E. M. WARD, R.A.

65 The Execution of Montrose

J. WARD, R A.
66 Cows and Calves 2

O WEBER.
67 Cattle at Pasture, Sevenoaks

J. W. WHYMPER.
68 The Thames near Windsor

SIR D. WILKIE, R A.
69 The Visit to the Nurse

S DE WILDE.
70 Jack Banister

L J WOOD.
71 Caub on the Rhine

W WYLD.
72 The Fruit Market, Venice

W WYLD.
73 Baderes de Bigorre

PICTURES.

74 A Valley Scene, with sheep
75 Grapes; a Coast Scene, View of a House; and a Female Head   4

MRS. ARNOLD.

76 Going Home

G. BARRET.

77 Windsor Castle moonlight

B BLAKE.

78 Interior of a Larder, with dead game

R P BONE.

79 A Lady and a Child in a Garden

L. F. G. CATTERMOLE

80 The Dead Warrior

CROME

81 A Woody Landscape, with figures

W. J. CROYDON

82 Winter. Great Park, Windsor

J DANBY
83 PEEL CASTLE, Isle of Man

W. DANIELL, R A
84 THE HINDOO GIRL'S OFFERING

FREEZOR
85 STREET BLOSSOMS; and the Companion   2

FREEZOR.
86 A PEASANT MOTHER AND CHILD

H. FUSELI, R A.
87 THE PRINCE OF WALES APPEARING TO THE CONSPIRATORS

H. FUSELI, R A
88 SATURN AND MINERVA

H FUSELI R A.
89 SIN RECEIVING THE KEY OF HELL FROM DEATH

H. FUSELI, R A
90 TWO SUBJECTS OF FIGURES   2

J GLOVER
91 A RIVER SCENE, with bridge and cows

E. HARGITT.

92 THE ROAD BY THE SEA

F. D HARDY

93 THE CRASH
Exhibited at the International Exhibition, 1872

E HAYES, R.H.A.

94 ROUGH WATER — *Smith*

R HILDER.

95 A LANDSCAPE — *Baker*

J HOLLAND

96 THE RIALTO—*circle* — *Tooth.*

J HOLLAND, 1860

97 VIEW OF VENICE, with the Dogana — *do*

H. HOWARD, R.A.

98 BURNS AND HIGHLAND MARY

SIR E LANDSEER, R.A.

99 A HIGHLANDER ON A GREY HORSE — *Shepherd*

F PAGE.

100 REFRESHING THE INNER MAN

W. TURNER.

101 A Landscape

J WARD, R.A.

102 Portrait of a Dog

J MOLENAER

103 A Carousal

UNKNOWN

104 Portrait of Shakespeare

105 Portraits of a Dutch Lady and Gentleman, dated 1631—a a pair—ovals

106 Innocence

107 Head of Christ

CANALETTO

108 The Church of S Maria della Salute, and the Dogana, Venice

D. TENIERS

109 A Harvest Field

The following are the Property of A LADY.

ENGRAVINGS—*Framed.*

110 The opening of the 6th seal, after J Martin, by Phillips
111 Interiors of the House of Commons   2

PICTURES.
PORTRAITS

112 THE RT HON C J FOX   *Graves*
113 A GENTLEMAN, temp Charles II

T. GAINSBOROUGH, R A

114 A WOODY LANDSCAPE, with ruined tower, a wood-cutter and grey horse in the foreground—*see note on back*   *Colnaghi*

R WILSON, R A

115 A WOODY LANDSCAPE, with farm buildings, peasants, and cows

W SHAYER, SEN

116 THE FARM
Exhibited

J GLOVER

117 A GRAND RIVER SCENE IN CUMBERLAND, with cattle and sheep

DE WIT

118 FIGURES AT A FOUNTAIN

HORREMANS

119 A Village Scene, with peasants and dog

LOTENS

120 A Forest Scene, with figures

J WEENIX

121 A Garden Scene, with a dead horse, a cock, partridges and fruit

CAMPIDOGLIO

122 Autumn

FINIS

CPSIA information can be obtained at www.ICGtesting.com
Printed in the USA
LVOW11s0607180913

352941LV00008B/97/P